Fire Trucks
on the Move

Judith Jango-Cohen

Lerner Publications Company
Minneapolis

To the firefighters of Burlington, Massachusetts

Lerner Publications Company
A division of Lerner Publishing Group, Inc.
241 First Avenue North
Minneapolis, MN 55401 U.S.A.

Website address: www.lernerbooks.com

Library of Congress Cataloging-in-Publication Data

Jango-Cohen, Judith.
    Fire trucks on the move / by Judith Jango-Cohen.
       p.   cm. — (Lightning bolt books™ – Vroom-vroom)
    Includes index.
    ISBN 978-0-7613-6023-0 (lib. bdg. : alk. paper)
    1. Fire engines—Juvenile literature. I. Title.
    TH9372.J3525 2011
    628.9'259—dc22   2009039740

Manufactured in the United States of America
1 — BP — 7/15/10

Contents

Fire Trucks

WHEE-OOO! WHEE-OOO!
What is making such a
loud sound?

That loud sound is the siren of a fire truck.

The siren is on the front of the truck.

A fire truck carries firefighters to a fire. What else does a fire truck carry?

This crew fights fires in Virginia.

A fire truck also carries tools called gear. The truck is like a toolbox on wheels.

This is some of the gear that you'll find in a fire truck.

Look! A house is on fire!
WHEE-OOO! WHEE-OOO!
Sirens blast, and lights flash.
A fire truck is on the way.

Does a fire truck speed away like a race car?

Fire trucks leave
the station on
the way to a fire.

No! A fire truck is too heavy to race safely. A heavy truck must move at a normal speed.

SANTA PAULA FIRE - RESCUE

57

82

Fire trucks drive at normal speeds to help keep firefighters safe.

The Gear

Soon the fire truck is at the fire. Firefighters open the truck's big doors. The gear is stored behind these doors.

Axes can chop burning walls. Pike poles can poke. Pike poles are special tools used to poke holes in a burning building.

A fire truck carries axes, pike poles, and other firefighting tools.

The holes they make let out smoke. How do firefighters work in smoke and not choke?

Firefighters chop a hole in the roof of a burning house.

A fire truck carries tanks of air.

Firefighters help one another put on their air tanks.

Firefighters wear air tanks on their backs. They breathe this air instead of smoke.

Drowning Fires

A fire truck also carries long water hoses. Water flows through the hoses.

This fire truck has two different

SPLASH! SIZZLE! The fire fizzles out. But what if a fire is up high?

A tower truck has
a ladder on top.
The ladder is
heavy. It could
tip the truck.

Outriggers must go down before the ladder goes up. Outriggers are parts that hold the truck safely in place.

Outriggers help the truck stay balanced.

A firefighter moves the ladder with levers. Levers turn the ladder and make it go up.

A firefighter moves the ladder of a tower truck.

20

This tower truck ladder is as long as two trucks.

At the top of the ladder is a big bucket. Firefighters can stand inside it.

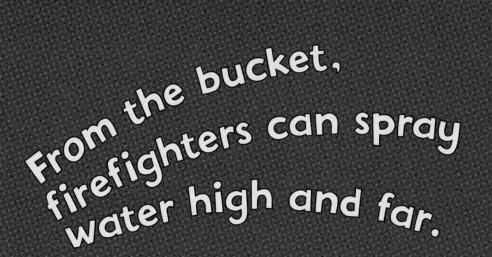

From the bucket,
firefighters can spray
water high and far.

Firefighters shoot
powerful streams of
water from the top
of a tower truck.

Heading Home

The fire is out. The fire truck is heading back to the station.

This fire truck pulls into the station's garage.

How many wheels carry the firefighters and their gear?

This tower truck has two wheels in front and eight in back. Ten wheels move ladders, axes, tanks, hoses, and poles.

Each side of the back of this fire truck has four wheels.

This big toolbox
is ready to roll!

Fire Truck Diagram

bucket

ladder

hose

light

siren

wheel

gear

outrigger

Fun Facts

- Some fire trucks carry their own water in big tanks.

- Some fire departments paint their trucks yellow to make them easy to see at night.

- A tower truck's ladder can be 100 feet (30 meters) long. That's tall enough to reach the eighth floor of a building.

- A fire truck can cost as much as forty cars!

- Early fire trucks were pulled by horses. They carried firefighters and gear in the days before engines.

This crew fought fires in Wenatchee, Washington, around 1911.

Glossary

bucket: a place at the end of a fire truck's ladder where firefighters stand to spray a high fire

gear: tools that a fire truck carries

lever: a control that moves a fire truck's ladder

outrigger: a part that holds a tower truck safely on the ground when its ladder is up

pike pole: a tool used to poke holes in a burning building

siren: a horn that makes a warning noise

tank: a container that holds air for a firefighter to breathe

tower truck: a fire truck that has a ladder

Further Reading

Brecke, Nicole, and Patricia M. Stockland. *Cars, Trucks, and Motorcycles You Can Draw.* Minneapolis: Millbrook Press, 2010.

Enchanted Learning: Fire Trucks and Firefighters
http://www.enchantedlearning.com/themes/firetruck.shtml

Lindeen, Mary. *Fire Trucks.* Minneapolis: Bellwether Media, 2007.

Lyon, George Ella. *Trucks Roll!* New York: Atheneum Books for Young Readers, 2007.

Sparky the Fire Dog
http://www.sparky.org

Teitelbaum, Michael. *If I Could Drive a Fire Truck!* New York: Scholastic, 2001.

Index

Photo Acknowledgments

The images in this book are used with the permission of: © travis manley/Shutterstock Images, p. 1; © Joy Brown/Shutterstock Images, p. 2; © Stephen St. John/National Geographic/Getty Images, p. 4; © Bob Peterson/UpperCut Images/Getty Images, pp. 5, 17; © Ariel Skelley/The Image Bank/Getty Images, p. 6; © Dylan D. Dog/Alamy, p. 7; © Dale A Stork/Shutterstock Images, p. 8; © fotog/Getty Images, p. 9; © Timothy Swope/TRANSTOCK, Inc./Alamy, p. 10; © Peter Hanson/Shutterstock.com, p. 11; © JAM WORLD IMAGES/Alamy, p. 12; © Blue Shadows/Alamy, pp. 13, 15; © Tim Pleasant/Shutterstock Images, p. 14; © Katrina Brown/Shutterstock Images, p. 16; © Enigma/Alamy, p. 18; © Mike Brake/Shutterstock Images, p. 19; © Homeros/Shutterstock Images, p. 20; © Robert Warren/Stone/Getty Images, p. 21; © Michael Doolittle/Alamy, p. 22; © Tommy Flynn/Photonica/Getty Images, p. 23; © Christina Richards/Shutterstock Images, p. 24; © Ryasick/Dreamstime.com, p. 25; © fotosearch/Photolibrary, p. 26; © M.Uptegrove/Shutterstock Images, p. 27; Library of Congress (LC-USZ62-46001), p. 28; (C) Laura Westlund/Independent Picture Service, p. 29; © iStockphoto.com/Travis Manley, p. 30; © iStockphoto.com/David H. Lewis, p. 31 (top); © iStockphoto.com/Robert Kylio, p. 31 (bottom).

Front cover: istockphoto.com/ryasick (top); Hans Lippert/Imagebroker.net /Photolibrary (bottom).